THE SKY FALLS TWICE

Lora Ward Clark

Copyright © 2020 Lora Ward-Clark

All rights reserved. No part of this publication may be reproduced, distributed, or transmitted in any form or by any means, including photocopying, recording, or other electronic or mechanical methods, without the prior written permission of the publisher, except in the case of brief quotations embodied in critical reviews and certain other noncommercial uses permitted by copyright law.

Publisher's Note:

All Scripture quotations, unless otherwise indicated, are taken from the Holy Bible, New International Version®, NIV®. Copyright ©1973, 1978, 1984, 2011 by Biblica, Inc.® Used by permission of Zondervan. All rights reserved worldwide. www.zondervan.com The "NIV" and "New International Version" are trademarks registered in the United States Patent and Trademark Office by Biblica, Inc.®

Library of Congress Control Number: 2020920240
Copyright: @2020 by Lora Ward-Clark. All rights reserved.
Paperback ISBN: 978-1-7355766-0-2
E book ISBN: 978-1-7355766-1-9

Cover Design: Austin Weatherspoon | AustinGraphix | Austingraphix@gmail.com
Formatted by: Success Dealers International, LLC
Author: Lora Ward-Clark

Ordering Information:

Special discounts are available on quantity purchases by corporations, associations, and others. For details, contact the publisher. For orders by U.S. trade bookstores and wholesalers contact the publisher at wardfind@gmail.com.

Printed in the United States of America.

Dedication

This book is dedicated to my mother, children, and grandchildren. To everyone who is navigating through the stages of grief after the death of a family member, close friend, or colleague. This too SHALL PASS!

In loving memory of my dad and husband who are the inspiration behind the book.

Acknowledgements

I would first like to thank God for giving me the opportunity to impact lives. Without God, none of this would have been possible.

I would like to thank my sister, Lena, who has been by my side since the death of my husband, with hugs so tight I can feel you trying to take my pain away. Your lovely smiles and daily phone calls get me through the day. My sister Felicia, for always thinking of me when she needed a walking partner. Those walks allowed me to exhale long enough to get back to writing. My sister. Lene, and friends, Karen, and Dee, who came all the way from Delaware to support me through the death of my husband and have been supportive in every way possible.

I would like to thank my son for being my rock and a shoulder to cry on without judgment. I remember that fateful day when my husband had the seizure and I called him on my way to the hospital with a trembling voice saying, "I think David is dying." Your response was, "mom what do you need me to do?" You always encourage me to complete projects and never give up. You are always in my corner cheering me on even when it didn't make sense, you supported me anyway. Running errands and assisting with your grandmother all while taking care of your own family; it doesn't go unnoticed.

I want to thank my daughter, Neasa, for her many calls. She always knows when something is wrong from my voice or facial expressions. Thanks for being vigilant and a listening ear when needed. You are always my cheerleader and giving me those wellness checks.

I want to thank my mom for showing strength and what it takes to get through the death of a spouse. Thank you for always being my cheerleader and understanding when I need space. I know I isolate myself but it's all a part of the process.

I want to thank my grandbabies, E'myah, Ezra, Justin, Elonora, and Aulora, for their unconditional love that fills the void. They always put a smile on their Grammy's face.

I would like to thank all of my family, friends (near and far) and co-workers who showed love during those trying times in my life. No matter how big or small the role may have been, it never went unnoticed.

I would like to thank my coach, Tiphane` Purnell of Success Dealers International, LLC for her patience and commitment to my project. Your commitment made me determined and not give up.

I would like to thank Austin Weatherspoon for my awesome book cover and website designer.

TABLE OF CONTENTS

INTRODUCTION	1
IT'S ME	5
CODE BLUE	15
IT'S ME AGAIN	23
NOT QUITE YOUR SUPERWOMAN	31
HEALING PROCESS	37
PROJECTS	46
THE INVISIBLE STRING	53
IN SEARCH OF HEALING	71
CONCLUSION	80
APPENDIX:	82
AFFIRMATIONS:	85
WHAT TO LOOK FOR IN A THERAPIST	87
ABOUT THE AUTHOR	88

Matthew 5:4, Blessed are those who mourn, for they will be comforted.

INTRODUCTION

When we are hurt, we may carry the stench of betrayal, pain and lies with us. It can and will haunt us, follow us, and hold us back. But what if we are able to shed our suffering? What if our hurt didn't hold us back after all? I remember being an eight-year-old girl and experiencing the death of my friend who was also eight years old. Imagine an eight-year-old girl being told she was never going to see her best friend again. It was not because she was attending a different school, moving to another city, state or even another country, but that she has gone to heaven, like your 60-year-old grandmother. How should an eight-year-old think? I could probably accept the fact that she went to another school or relocated to a different state, but not the numbness I felt when my mom explained to me that my friend DIED, not even realizing or understanding that death is final when it comes to a child or my best friend. You experience death with your first goldfish that you win from the neighborhood carnival, but you don't think anything of it except child's play. We don't really understand grief when our goldfish dies, because your parents tell you that they will get you another. When you get home from school, it's like magic, "POOF!", you have a new goldfish floating in the same fishbowl with the same name *Goldie* or *Fishy* and you're happy again. But what about those children whose parents, for whatever reason, aren't able to replace the goldfish. That child asks questions like" where is Fishy"? and get answers like "He's in Fishy Heaven." and they ask, "Where is that?" When these questions arise, it is important that you take this time to talk with the child about death and grief because if you don't, it will impact them as adults. Pets are an important part of people's families and losing a pet can stir up the same emotions and grief as when your mom, dad, grandma, or any close relative dies. So, it's important to talk to a child about grief, because it can affect how they deal with grief as an adult.

Grief is deep sorrow, especially caused by someone's death. We all must encounter death at some point. It may be a close friend, relative, or colleague. Death affects everyone in different ways depending on the relationship one had with the deceased. Grief can be triggered by many different events that may take place in one's life such as divorce, dismissal from a job, change in financial state, or imprisonment, to name a few. Researchers say that there are different stages of grief which are shock, denial, guilt, anger, bargaining, depression, and acceptance. Some individuals may work through grief through professional counseling, others may find comfort through some type of chemical substance, others may find comfort through spirituality. No matter how you decide to deal with the grief in your life, the overall outcome is to be healthier in the end. Many people try to heal from the outer to the inner. It's just like exercising where an individual looks at what they want the outside to look like, but they are forgetting about the inside. It all starts with a state of mind and when you are grieving, your mental isn't in one piece, so you may put on a mask so the outside can look or appear to be all intact. I understand how this works! I was in the same boat thinking I had it together, but my inner was a hot mess. You think that you encounter the event in your life that causes the grief once and then it's over. The event tends to follow you and is triggered every time something happens in your life that allows those memories or feelings to arise. This is my story. I walked alone for many years, but I don't want you to walk alone so I will walk with you through my book. Grab my hand as I help you through THIS JOURNEY.

Scripture:

2 Corinthians 10:3-5: For though we live in the world, we do not wage war as the world does. The weapons we fight with are not the weapons of the world. On the contrary, they have divine power to demolish strongholds. We demolish arguments and every pretension that sets itself up against the knowledge of God, and we take captive every thought to make it obedient to Christ.

IT'S ME

CHURCH, CHURCH, CHURCH!!!! Growing up with a strong faith background, everything revolved around church. No matter the situation, it was prayed about. Sometimes, I don't want to pray about it. I want to act out, I want to smack a couple of faces and scream and shout without being looked at as crazy. Maybe I am CRAZY for believing that there is a higher power when it's foggy and it seems like I'm not being heard. I can't believe I spent my life, day and night, in church praying, fasting and shouting, shut in after shut in, Sunday school, Bible study, prayer night, revivals six weeks at a time and traveling to another state for summer vacation when it turns out to be another church service all over again.

Learning the Lord's Prayer; *Our Father, who art in heaven, hallowed be thy name, thy kingdom come, thy will be done on earth as it is in heaven.* It's me sitting here thinking back to when I was a little girl praying to God to heal my friend from an illness at eight years old. We used to play dolls when we visited one another. We were two little girls old at heart. We went to school together and played together. One day, as I entered the classroom, my friend wasn't there. When I asked my mom about it, she said that she was sick in the hospital. As an eight-year-old child, I continued on with life as normal. Time went by and my friend's seat at school was still empty. When I asked my mom about her again, she repeated that she was still in the hospital. Finally, one day, my mom told me that my friend will not be coming to school because she went to heaven like my grandmother. My eight-year-old self-rebutted that kids don't die, only old people. My mom explained that she was really sick and that she was in a better place. I remember attending her funeral with my brother because my parents were out of town at the time. That was the scariest time of my life going to a funeral without my parents, asking my brother questions he couldn't answer. You ask how an eight-year-old girl bounces back from such trauma. Does she get therapy, or does she continue life as if nothing took place. I continued life as normal, found a new friend and moved on. Is that healthy you ask? Probably not, but that's how it happened.

Thinking on this prayer, I ask, "is this God's will to have me become a friendless and fatherless child?" DADDY with his deep dark skin complexion, deep curly locks of hair, and his strong 5'7 stature. My daddy would move any mountain and tear down any barrier for me. He was my hero without a cape. My hero was ill and losing weight at a rapid pace. I prayed and prayed that my daddy would be healed. Every time we went to church, we prayed for my daddy. Before I went to bed, I prayed for my dad's healing.

God, why did you have to take my dad and leave me with so many unanswered questions and no direction? Why would you take my daddy? God, he was my biggest supporter, and you took him away right before my high school graduation. God, you allowed him to be there for everyone else except me. It was very hard for me to enjoy specific milestones or events in my life wondering if daddy was proud of me.

He wasn't at my first big ball due to his illness. My dad was diagnosed with lung cancer my junior year in high school. I remember getting dressed for my Debutante Ball, going into the bedroom where he was lying in a hospital bed and asking him questions like "Do you like my hair daddy?" There was no response, just a nod of his head. I went to the ball all excited and I remember looking around at all the young ladies as we were laughing and having fun. Once it was time to get dressed and line up to be presented to society, I proceeded to the line in the foyer with the other girls with mixed emotions. I stood in line, all smiles, listening for my name to be announced and then I finally heard it, *Lora Mardell Ward*. I entered the arch and as my bio was being read (walking down the aisle), I turned to walk towards my parents and it hit me that my dad wasn't here to present me; my brother was the stand in. I love my brother; however, I wanted this special night to be with my dad. My first dance was the waltz with my brother at the Omni Netherland Hotel ballroom. It was an elegant black-tie affair in the month of December. We were all dressed in our white ball gowns with long gloves. This was the moment we were waiting for and I couldn't wait for it to be over. I smiled for pictures and mingled with friends and family, but I couldn't wait to get home to show my daddy my ball gown. I hurried home after the event so my dad could see me in my ball gown. Like a little daddy's girl on Easter Sunday spinning around in her Easter dress, I asked my frail weak dad how I looked and with all the strength he could muster, he nodded his head in approval. Being pleased with the response, I went to my room and changed into something more comfortable. As a teenager, I still thought my dad was invincible, and he would always be here, especially for my senior year's events and any other events in my life for that matter.

The next week was Christmas and we always have a large family gathering at our parent's house with my siblings and their families. It's always such an exciting time singing songs, playing with my nieces and nephews, taking pictures, exchanging gifts and of course, eating the plethora of food. I look over and see my dad sitting in his chair in the living room with very little energy. This saddened me because he was fading away right before my young eyes. Christmas comes and goes, still not thinking that my dad (my hero) wasn't going to pull through this illness because he was such a strong guy. New Year's Eve rolls around and, of course you guessed it, we were hustling and bustling about the house trying to get ready for church before 11pm. We are in church all night long until daylight hit the next morning. The church was packed like a can of sardines with *the fragrance* of sweat and a mixture of perfumes. People were sitting and standing in every corner of the church shouting hallelujah, dancing, singing, and preaching all to the glory of God. The night moves along and it's about 4am and you start seeing people leaving the sanctuary to go to the kitchen to prepare the breakfast buffet. An hour goes by and the next aroma you smell is Bacon. How can you stay focused in church with the fresh BACON aroma seeping into the SANCTUARY? I felt like the dog on that Beggin Strip commercial running around displaying excitement for some bacon. Ok, I'm focused now. After church service, everyone makes their way to the dining hall to eat breakfast. You know how it is when your family comes to your house for an event and everyone is eating, laughing and being merry and then they leave. What happens next? You and your siblings are left behind cleaning the kitchen and putting things away. Our church family was left to clean the kitchen and dining hall which usually meant we didn't get home until like mid-morning NEW YEARS DAY. When we returned home mid- morning the next day, it seemed as if my dad was getting weaker as the days went by. He was sleeping more and more and no longer had the energy to take care of the normal everyday duties of life, which meant my mom had to be responsible for handling my dad's hygiene needs.

I was studying to become a Nurse Assistant in high school, so every day when I came home from school, I could see that my daddy was slowly slipping away. I watched as the signs of death that we learned in class unraveled right before my young eyes. I saw the staring of the eyes, the shallow breathing and even though they teach us that hearing is the last to go. I had no way of knowing if my daddy heard anything I said. No matter what I said, he didn't respond with a simple yes or no or one of his infamous sly remarks. At that point, reality was setting in. I knew that I had to be self-sufficient because my hero and provider wouldn't be here to protect and rescue me like he was for my siblings and everyone else. He wouldn't be here to enjoy any of my accomplishments, birth of my children, graduations, marriage etc. I was right because on January 8th, 1986, my dad lost his battle with Lung Cancer.

The Debutante ball was just the beginning of the many important events that my dad would miss in my life. It's my senior year in high school. What am I going to do now? When everyone was jubilant about senior year, I was on this roller coaster ride with unanswered questions in my mind still going through everyday life with a smile on my face because I knew there were things I needed to do. No matter how many times I tried to convince myself by saying, "it's ok, he's with God in heaven and he's looking down on you every day smiling saying *good job*", it wasn't comforting and didn't ease the pain and hurt of a 17 year old teenage girl with all the other unwanted emotions that were present in my life; the emotions I had towards God. I was angry with God but growing up in church, I knew I wasn't supposed to curse God or use His name in vain. But I was angry that my dad would not walk me down the aisle, see my children and grandchildren, tell me how proud he was of me graduating from high school and college, see me buying my first house and my first car and achieve my dreams. Being so cautious not to go against the things I have been taught regarding how to respond to GOD during this time of confusion left me stuck. I was still supposed to believe in a GOD that no matter how many prayers we sent up; we still fell short when it came to healing my dad. I was supposed to believe that the God of the UNIVERSE never fails but my dad never received his healing here on earth. Did he receive his reward which is being reunited with God in HEAVEN?

With my dad's absence in my crucial years, <u>and the separation anxiety</u> never <u>gave me</u> the desire or the urgency to get married, have children, or want to achieve any of the normal milestones in adulthood. I was just completing the necessary survival task of life. However, as an adult and a believer in Christ, I now understand that my dad's healing was not to take place on earth, it may have been to be with the Lord. I had to understand that his healing was according to his faith and relationship with God not mine. Who knows, maybe I wouldn't have become the independent person that I am. Hey, **IT'S ME**.

Your Journey
It's You

Scripture:

Psalms 121:1-3, I will lift my eyes to the hills, from whence cometh my help. My help cometh from the Lord, which made heaven and earth. He will not suffer my feet to be moved: he that keepeth me will not slumber,

CODE BLUE

I was watching television when he began to cry. I went to his crib, picked him up only to notice that he was having some labored breathing. With every breath he took, his little chest would rise and collapse as if he were struggling to get enough air through his airways. Panicking, I called the doctor's office, and the call went to the answering service. After taking the information, the answering service informed me to take my infant son to the emergency room. I immediately got my baby dressed and rushed out of the house and drove to the emergency room. Although the hospital is just around the corner from where I lived, it felt as if I was driving miles away. Upon arrival, we were rushed to an exam room and they immediately began assessing my infant son by taking his vitals, drawing blood, doing a complete work up, and administering oxygen. As a young mother all alone and frightened, I began to pray to God as I anxiously waited for my infant son's test results. I prayed that all the test results came back normal and my infant son be discharged. Well once again that was not my story. The nurse returned to the exam room looking at my jovial little baby and responded that "he doesn't look as sick as the blood gases results show". That isn't information you give to a twenty-six-year-old new mom about her first child to marinate with and leave the room. No explanation. Now I'm really in panic mode and thinking, "is that a good or bad thing?" The doctor enters the room and explains that my four-month old baby will be admitted to the hospital with a respiratory illness (RSV). He explained that it is a common cold but with my infant son being so little it's difficult for him to cough the phlegm out of his bronchial tubes, so it sits there and obstructs his breathing. He assured me that my son would be fine. My infant son was admitted to a hospital room with five other babies with Respiratory Syncytial Virus (RSV). I'm not a doctor but it seems to me that it would be contagious, and my infant son should be in isolation since he's so young. Well as the evening progressed, my son was getting a little fussy, so I decided to feed him. As I was feeding my infant son his bottle, I looked to see how much milk he had drunk. As soon as I went to burp him, he vomited like an erupting volcano. Trying not to panic, I casually pulled the call light and the voice on the other end responded, "May I help you?" I responded, "my son vomited, and I need something to clean it up". The voice on the other end responded, "I'm sending in your nurse." While waiting on the nurse, I returned my son to the crib, and I began to use the paper towels in the room to clean up the vomit. The nurse entered the room with a baffled look or her face. She looked at the vast amount of vomit and immediately began to check his vitals. She urgently pulled the call light and said, "I need you to call a CODE BLUE." I have worked as a Telecommunication Operator at the hospital since the age of nineteen, so I was familiar with the action that's getting ready to happen. I'm usually the one on the other end of the telephone paging the CODE BLUE team to respond to the emergency. The shoe was now on the other foot. I'm the one being whisked out of the patient's room and being asked to wait in the waiting area. My mind races with uncertainties not quite sure how to react or feel. So, I frantically picked up the phone and called my son's pediatrician, who's a close family friend at home. I began to explain what was happening and his response was that his other line was ringing and it's most likely the hospital informing him of the emergency. So, I sat and waited as I watched people race in and out of my infant son's hospital room. The next thing I saw was my infant son in a hospital bed, hooked up to machines and being whisked away followed by a team of white jackets and scrubs moving like a locomotive at a very high speed. The doctor approached me and explained my son had just gone into respiratory arrest and he was being moved to the ICU. He then asked, "Do you need to call anyone?" If there was ever a time that I thought I knew Jesus it was now. I knew that I had to call on Jesus for myself in this time of need. I remembered that your healing is connected to your faith. Well since my infant son couldn't verbally respond to God, the results of this healing depended on my faith. I looked up and I said, "God I know you didn't give me this precious jewel just to take him away from me." I called my prayer warriors my momma and my godmother. If anyone could get a prayer through, those sisters could. I should know; I have watched them shake up a couple of people, throw water all in the air falling on those fresh hairstyles and grease enough people with holy oil all in the name of Jesus. Days go by and I have spent days and nights in the hospital with my son hooked up to the machines and tubes going every which way from his arms to his mouth. My son lay in the ICU for fourteen days and I didn't miss a moment by his side. Scary moment!!! That's a time when I had to pull on my faith and put it into action. Pulling from all those things I learned from prayer meetings, bible studies and church services. Praying without ceasing, fasting, worshiping God even when you didn't think he was near, and praising him through the trials and tribulations. Needless to say, those were the longest fourteen days of my life. Spending the night at the hospital, praying with hope for God to deliver my son and He did just that. He was finally discharged. That was a sigh of relief and a blessing in itself to have my son home and returning to some type of life's normalcy.

Moving forward, my son has grown to be a healthy little boy and at the ripe little age of four, I decided that we were moving to Delaware. It would be us against the Delaware world which was very small. Life was good. I had a decent job, earned my Bachelor of Science degree in Education, and purchased my first home. I was active in my church working with the youth and doing outreach. Life is good or so I thought. We were living our best life until one day, I received a call from my son's father in Cincinnati informing me that one of my best friends was recently killed in a car accident. In shock and disbelief, I called her brother and he informed me that the information was true my songbird was now singing in heaven. You deal with the loss and move forward. Years go by and death was like an avalanche in my life. My nephew was killed in a car accident, then two weeks later, my younger cousin's daughter died from an aneurysm, six months later, my nephew was shot and killed, two weeks to a month, my godmother died. This was so overwhelming and a lot to sink in and try to understand why these things were happening. That would be four young life's taken, I began to wonder, "Lord whose attention are you trying to get all of this going on in one family. Was it the entire family, was it the parents that were directly affected by the deaths or was IT ME AGAIN?" So, I began to look at the things that were going on in my life and wondered if there was a family curse. I decided to ask God what's next. I began to search for answers in the Bible (**B**asic **I**nstructions **B**efore **L**eaving **E**arth), praying and fasting more. Then I cried out to God to reveal to me what needs to change in me and in my family. Time waits for no man and life moves on rather you want it to or not.

Once again, we return to life's normalcy. My son voiced his opinion of attending college in Ohio, so in the summer of 2010, I relocated my son to Ohio to live with his father and attend high school to establish residency for college. Two years later, I relocated to Ohio to ensure my son completed high school. Upon completion of high school, he was accepted and attended Shawnee State University in Portsmouth Ohio. I was excited to be free from the responsibility of others. While he was away at college, exploring and having his little adventures, I was having my own little adventures.

So, my mom needed work on her house and in the process, I was introduced to a contractor who swept me off my feet. Well not at first. He was a very nice guy, and we were spending time together at Home Depot as he gathered materials to finish my mom's basement. As time went on, we became fond of one another and became an item. We graduated from spending time at the Home Depot to traveling to different cities, attending family gatherings, going bowling, fishing, playing pool and late-night walks. We had spent time enjoying each other's company, telling each other jokes and making each other laugh. This man could make my heart stop beating. Call a CODE BLUE and bring me back to life all with one SMILE!!!!!

Your Journey
Panic Mode

Scripture:

Philippians 4:8 Finally, brothers and sisters, whatever is true, whatever is noble, whatever is right, whatever is pure, whatever is lovely, whatever is admirable- if anything is excellent or praiseworthy- think about such things.

IT'S ME AGAIN

Lord, it's me again, as I maneuver through this journey called life. Now, I have entered into adulthood without any grief counseling to learn the proper strategies to deal with the many encounters of people dying (i.e. friends, family, co-workers, etc..). The loss of loved ones has left me with many unanswered questions and broken pieces to mend. I was left with scars and open wounds that were hidden by a fifty-nine-cent bandage. If that bandage were to be removed, it would reveal the many scars and unhealed wounds that were left behind by my unwanted guest called grief. Grief shows its ugly face as soon as I think that I'm going to have my fairytale ending; my happily ever after. God, I met this guy that I believe is the one. He makes me happy and makes my heart skip several beats. One day, while sitting up and talking he asked me to marry him. Before I responded yes, I asked if he had gone through the proper chain of command. So, he asked my mom, my son, and my brother for my hand in marriage. We were excited about making plans for our future, until one day, while talking, he says that he thinks he might have lung cancer. I'm thinking "well who just throws that out in a conversation as if you were offering someone a piece of gum." I asked, "what would make you think that?" He responds that it hurts when he takes deep breaths. We agreed to go to the emergency room after church. So, after church, we picked up his sister and went to Mercy Health emergency room on Queen City Avenue. This is where we were given the dreadful diagnosis and confirmation that he had lung cancer. That night, we went home, and we cried together. After the initial shock and tears, we decided to face this thing on. So, we made appointments, went for treatments, and took advantage of support groups. As if that wasn't enough, we continued to make wedding arrangements still excited about our nuptials. We picked our venue, he finally decided on my ring after having purchased two other rings previously. We chose his suit and suits for his groom's men, the dresses for the women, and finally my wedding (jumpsuit) dress. We were putting the finishing touch for our big day. Invitations were sent, save the date and people were slowly RSVP. Then there comes another blow to the chest and the heart. A week before our big day, David was stricken with bacteria pneumonia and hospitalized for two weeks. Praying to God that he will be discharged before our big day didn't happen. Instead, the doctors were adamant about us reserving the hospital's chapel for our wedding ceremony. So, they sent the chaplain into David's hospital room to discuss reserving the chapel. Disappointed with mixed emotions. I had one of my infamous temper tantrums that would probably be the biggest ever, screaming "I am not getting married in the hospital's chapel. I won't get married at all". Then I looked over at my fiancé and saw the look on his face. I thought how selfish I was. My fiancé was laying there in a hospital bed on oxygen not even sure of the outcome, and I was whining about a wedding ceremony, when the focus should have been his health and the love we have for one another. Our wedding day was slowly approaching, and my fiancé was still on a very high dose of oxygen. The Dr. informed us that he would not grant David medical clearance to travel to the venue because of the amount of oxygen he needed for survival at that time. Needless to say, the day before my wedding, we needed to have a plan B incorporating the hospital chapel as our wedding venue. While decorating the venue, I asked the director if they had a way to livestream the wedding. Plan B was in full effect to stream the wedding live from the chapel to the venue where the guests would be able to view the ceremony. This was the only way to carry on with the ceremony without canceling. The wedding was beautiful. It was ironic that we were getting married in a garden and the chapel at hospital was located near a garden. The hospital's staff assist my husband with getting dressed and getting to the chapel. We proceeded with the wedding and my husband was discharged two days later. Due to my husband's illness, we had to postpone the honeymoon till January. The honeymoon of his choice was to VEGAS. What happens in VEGAS stays in VEGAS! Ok I will share some information on social media. If you don't follow me on social media, then you won't know what happened in VEGAS.

We returned home from Vegas and continued life as normal. Then one day, David woke up complaining about stomach pain. This was new because my husband never complained. Whatever was ailing him blew over after a couple of days so we figured it must have been a stomach virus on something. That must have been late January or early February. Not knowing that the next 4 months, my husband would be gone forever. We were planning our next trip to Delaware, a cruise and the grandbabies' trip to Disney. Needless to say, those trips never happened.

It was the month of May and my daughter Neasa brought Ezra down for her annual grandparents' visit. We had so many activities to keep her occupied during her summer visit. We were not nearly prepared for the events that took place during her visit. She wasn't in the city twenty-four hours before her PAPA was admitted to the hospital with abdominal pains. This was becoming the norm. David gets dehydrated and is admitted for a couple of days then he's discharged. We returned home after his weeklong stay in the hospital to receive fluids and check his port. We had to change our summer itinerary due to David's health. Ezra and I will have to have fun without papa. Ezra wanted to play with her cousin E'myah who was in daycare. We received permission to pick E'myah up from daycare, stopped for ice cream and on to our grandparents' house we go to do arts and crafts. The girls and I were taking photos and playing on social media as papa watched. The summer was quickly passing, and Ezra's visit was coming to an end when the inevitable happened. Ezra and I were preparing for the day when David was lying down watching television when his body went limp. I have seen this once before my grandad died. They would have what the medical personnel refer to as syncope (temporary loss of consciousness caused by a drop in their blood pressure). I called his name, shook him and when he didn't respond, I quickly called 911 and explained the situation to the operator. While talking to the operator, I took our granddaughter downstairs to sit with my mom before the paramedics arrived. By the time the paramedics arrived, David had regained consciousness and was able to communicate. The paramedics put him on the stretcher and proceeded to put David in the ambulance to take him to the hospital. I quickly got dressed, combed my hair, and followed the ambulance to the hospital. When I arrived at the hospital, David was sitting up in the bed and was communicating with the nurses and everyone that came into the triage room. The doctor entered the room and explained that he had a syncopal episode and she wanted him to have a CT scan. I kissed my husband and we exchanged "I love you" and that was the last time I heard my husband speak.

<u>I will never hear him speak the words "I love you more today than yesterday but not as much as tomorrow".</u> I went to the waiting area to sit with my family until David returns to the room. The next thing I hear is my name being paged overhead to report to the CT scan area. Upon my arrival, I was met by a physician explaining to me that my husband has had another seizure during the CT scan and has to be intubated. People were hurrying about. Going to and fro working to save my husband's life. I'm reflecting back, thinking "God not again". I remember being in this position twenty-three years ago with my infant son. Thinking once again, "God why me." I prayed to God day and night to please heal my husband. My husband was intubated. I'm praying to God, please heal my husband. The doctors request another test and I'm still praying to God. I'm sitting by David's bedside, holding his hand, rubbing his forehead, speaking into his ears, and still praying to God. God please heal my husband and bring him back to me, so we can have our Happily Ever After. David was stabilized and admitted to ICU where he would be until the day when he takes his last breath. No matter how many times I prayed to God, my prayers again went unanswered. On June 12th, 2019, at 6:30am, my heart was broken once again. David died surrounded by his loving family and friends. I was angry with God for allowing me to feel this numbness and emptiness once again.

Your Journey
It's You Again

Scripture:

Matthew 11:28-30 "Come to me, all you who are weary and burdened, and I will give you rest. Take my yoke upon you and learn from me, for I am gentle and humble in heart, and you will find rest for your souls. For my yoke is easy and my burden is light."

NOT QUITE YOUR SUPERWOMAN

Blasting the song "I'm not your superwoman" in the background, I'm repeating in my mind that I can't be everything to everybody. I'm being pulled in every direction possible trying to please everyone. It has always been that way. I am a different breed. I'll get it done no matter what it takes. I am the mother, grandmother, the daughter, the sister, aunt, the teacher, the coach, and the friend.

It's Saturday morning and from the moment my feet hit the floor, I'm running for someone doing something, it doesn't matter which role I'm playing at the moment there is something that needs to be done. I wake up in the morning and put my cape on to fly from here to there. I'm cooking, cleaning, doing laundry, combing hair, watching babies. The telephone rings. I answer and the individual on the other end asks what I was doing. I respond "cooking, cleaning and doing laundry." Their response was, "Oh, I was going to ask if you could come over and watch the baby while I take a shower." You have got to be kidding me. I remember when my son was little, I would put him in the bathroom in his chair where he was visible, take my shower, brush my teeth, and start my day. Before I could even hang up, someone else is calling. "Auntie what are you doing?" I give the same reply. "I was wondering if you can run me to Walmart. I will give you gas money." I responded, "if I wasn't here what would have been your option for getting to Walmart". She says, "I would catch the bus". Well I guess you will be catching the bus. Yes, a small victory I said NOOOOOO!!!! It's the first Saturday of the month, the time is 9:35am, and I have to still cook breakfast for my mom, shower and be at a Gamma Phi Delta meeting by 10:30. I rush to the kitchen and look in the fridge to find something quick to cook so mom can eat breakfast before I leave the house. I whip up sausage links, eggs and toast, make her some tea and I go to the bathroom to take a quick shower, brush my teeth, grease myself up, get dressed and run out the door. Oops! I have to run back up the steps because I forget the necessary materials needed for the meeting. I get in the car and fly up Reading Road attempting to be on time for this meeting. Yes, I've made it. I have gone here for this person, taken this person there. Stop by a celebration and finally make it home. I'm exhausted so I get ready for bed. There is church in the morning. It's Sunday morning and I get ready to attend the 8am service. I rush out directly after service to return home to take mom to church. While she is at her church service, I usually run errands, do laundry, and cook dinner. Once I pick mom up from church and eat dinner, it's time to get ready for Monday morning.

The nightfall comes quickly and the next thing I know is it's Monday morning and the alarm is blasting throughout the room letting me know that it's 6am and time to start the day. I'm torn between getting out of bed and rolling over and putting the cover over my head to catch more ZZZs. Then I quickly grab the telephone to dial into the daily prayer line where I receive strength to start the day. My prayer circle has kept me grounded and has given me the strength to get out of bed and attack every windstorm one day at a time. When I am accepted into the prayer room, I hear someone ask if there were any prayer requests and I immediately knew it was Wednesday morning and Patty was going to take us to the throne of God. She's telling God thank you for waking us up on this side of time and not in eternity, thanking him for the things he's done and what he's going to do, then she goes into telling God how much we adore him, worship him and we give you all the glory and praise. She then proceeds to pray to God about the spoken and unspoken prayer requests. She ends the prayer. After that uplifting and powerful prayer, I am ready for any challenge. I can hit the ground running. Today starting the day of testing I'm thinking about all the roles I have to play testing proctor, meeting facilitator, trouble shooter, enumerator, Uber driver, counselor, and caregiver, but to name a few. I go into the bathroom to take care of my personal needs like showering and brushing my teeth. I can't take a long shower because I have to cook breakfast for my elderly mom before I leave the house for work. So, I get out of the shower, rush to the kitchen, put a pot of water on the stove to boil for grits. I turn on the tea kettle for her tea, I get the fruit and butter out of the refrigerator to slice the fruit and make toast. I rush to the bedroom to dress for work. The ensemble chosen for work today was a pair of tan khakis with black long-sleeved blouse. I spray my hair with rice water and brush it up into a ponytail. I tell my mom that her breakfast is ready and what's in the fridge for lunch.

Knowing that the time is drawing near for me to be out the door and in the car. I quickly run down the steps, open the front door, and lock the storm door behind me. I hurry to the car only to remember that my wallet is in my other work bag. So, I drop my work bag and everything else in the car and hurry up the steps to retrieve my wallet. I return to the car, make a quick sigh of relief and I'm on my way. I know that I have to play a role for so many people. This is how I stay grounded so I can wear all the many hats needed to support others.

Your Journey
The Power of Nooooo

Scripture:

Philippians 4:6-7: Do not be anxious about anything, but in every situation, by prayer and petition, with thanksgiving, present your requests to God. And the peace of God, which transcends all understanding, will guard your hearts and your minds in Christ Jesus

HEALING PROCESS

During your healing process, it is important to be able to identify your triggers. These triggers can be happening, and you do not even realize it's a trigger for you. You begin to stir up emotions when you are in a specific environment and not even understand why. Something I did was learn and understand what my triggers were. I knew that I didn't really feel comfortable at events where the focus was centered on couples, like when my cousin and nephew got married. Of course I was happy for them but I had to keep myself occupied during the reception because it was a trigger for me and if I wasn't moving, I would be overwhelmed with emotions and I didn't want to have long conversations with my friends or family members who were going to spend the conversation talking about what they are doing. *Don't want to hear it, see you, bye!* I don't want to seem bitter but those were my feelings. I don't think that people do this intentionally or even thinking that would be a trigger for me or anyone who has just lost their loved one. I'm sure our friends and family members are trying to help shift our focus away from the hurt we are feeling at the time. Thank you, however, it's not a good time to give me that particular invite, maybe invite me to a play or something. My cousin was really mindful of inviting me to events. I thank you for being considerate. I didn't want to become bitter or resentful of others, so I tried to keep my distance. As I reflect back on all the important milestones that my dad missed in my life, I may have had some bitterness because he was there for my siblings' important milestones like the birth of their children, school graduations and weddings just to name a few. I have unknowingly held these emotions bottled up inside all these years not knowing the effect it's had on my life. I had an epiphany when our family church had a revival honoring each of our legends throughout the week. I was asked to do a mini sermon before the main speaker. I knew this was part of my healing process because I had to be in a particular mindset before speaking to the people. I talked about character traits or FOO, Family of Origin. When you wonder why you do certain things in a certain way and then you see that trait in a family member. You then think to yourself, "that's where I get that from." Then I realized that some of these things I grew up doing could be the very thing that could be interfering with my healing and my blessings. After I spoke at the revival, I began to spend more personal time in my prayer closet. I began to pray and release some of the emotions I had towards God. I had to probably get out of a certain state of mind because God was not going to bless me in that place. After much prayer, listening to my healing process playlist and Sarah Jakes Roberts' Woman Evolve podcast. She was talking about putting some skin in the game. She said, "Put some skin in the game and God will plant the seed." So, I decided to put some skin in the game so I could come out of the dark place. This meant that I had to challenge vulnerability. I'm not sure about you guys, but I don't want to expose my brokenness, especially when people assume that I'm a strong individual. I remember when we were going to the funeral home for the family viewing before the service takes place. My mom, siblings and my friend, Karen from Delaware, were my support team for that day. As I was walking to the car, I remember my knees buckling and my sister Nessa caught me and she said to me "I know baby girl, but you can do this." I made it to the car where Karen was my chauffeur for the day. As we were riding down Reading Road, I remember letting out the loudest scream ever shouting, "I'M NOT OKAY, I'M NOT OKAY!" Karen, not knowing how to respond, says with her eyes looking straight ahead," It's okay, you don't have to be okay right now." That was her way of allowing me to be broken without judgement. Isn't that vulnerability being the real you? Society has groomed us into believing that we should" BEHAVE" a certain way and when our behavior doesn't fit into that box, you get strange looks or whispers for being your true self. Could this be the reason the Institute for Health Metrics and Evaluation reported an estimated 792 million people globally that live with a mental health disorder in 2017?[1] That's globally like one in ten people. I have six brothers and four sisters so that would mean one of us on any given day fits in these statistics. When I thought of it in that manner, I decided that I wasn't going to be a statistic so if being me didn't fit in the societal box, then I guess I was going to be the misfit. So, in November, I participated in the revival and talked about character traits and some of the darkness began to fade away; I could see some light shining through. It is December and time to celebrate the Christmas holiday. I wanted a change of scenery, so I went to Delaware and Pennsylvania to spend the holiday with my daughter and sister. I was smiling and allowing myself to feel happiness again. This was probably the first time I didn't feel empty inside. I was seeing my way through the darkness and more light was shining through. Then February strolled around, and my sisters and I went to Indiana to the Woman Evolve: Refuse to Lose Conference. God started revealing things about me that I had to release. I know you all didn't know this about me, but I can be a little bossy, controlling and can hold on to something forever. So as part of me letting go and starting the healing process. I started writing this book to release some of the things that I had going on that may lead to resentment and bitterness which could leave me broken inside. The life changing event I encountered, like David's death, left a void in my life and

---

[1]("A Discussion with Dr. Akmal Makhdum On Changing the "Mental Health Stigma" In Today's Society", 2020)

allowed me to relive other emotions that weren't healed; they were just buried. At that moment, I had to make the decision. What am I going to do to move forward? What are my next steps? It was then I remembered what Sarah Jakes Roberts said about minding her business and drinking her water. I did just that by releasing people and all their shenanigans and I was on my way to a brighter day. One day at a time. I had to let go of the teenage hurt from the death of my dad that merged with the hurt of losing my husband. Two separate life events that left me with resentment and bitterness.

Letting Go of Resentment & Bitterness Prayer

Heavenly Father, I come to you now in the Name of my Lord and Savior Christ Jesus. Heavenly Father, life seems so unjust, so unfair. The pain of rejection is almost more than I can bear. My past relationships have ended in strife, anger, rejection, resentment, and bitterness. Father help me to let go of all bitterness and resentment. You are the One Who binds up and heals the brokenhearted. I receive your anointing that breaks and destroys every yoke of bondage. I receive emotional healing by faith according to Your Word, Isaiah 53:5, "and with His stripes we are healed". I thank you for giving me the grace to stand firm until this process is complete. I acknowledge and I thank you for my wise Counselor, the Holy Spirit! Thank You for helping me work out my salvation with fear and trembling, for it is You, Father, who works in me to do your will and to act according to your good purpose. In the Name of Jesus, I choose to forgive those who have wronged me. I choose to live a life of forgiveness because you have forgiven me. With the help of the Holy Spirit, I get rid of all resentments, bitterness, rage, anger, brawling, and slander, along with every form of malice. I desire to be kind and passionate to others, forgiving them, just as through Christ, You forgave me. With the help of the Holy Spirit, I make every effort to live in peace with all men and to be holy, for I know that without holiness, no one will see you. I chose to receive and to not miss your grace and that no roots of resentment or bitterness grow up within me to cause trouble. I will watch and pray that I will not enter into temptation or cause others to stumble. Thank You, Heavenly Father that you watch over Your Word to perform it and that whom the Son has set free is free indeed. I declare that I have overcome resentment and bitterness by the Blood of the Lord Jesus Christ and by the word of my testimony. Amen.

Your Journey
Your Healing

Scripture:

Deuteronomy 31:8 The Lord himself goes before you and will be with you, he will never leave you nor forsake you. Do not be afraid; do not be discouraged

PROJECTS

People deal with separation anxiety and stress. I different ways some display unhealthy behaviors, some become introverts or stay to themselves and others may take on projects. I'm one who take on projects it may be an activity or people. You can go to someone's home, look around and see a different project in every corner. I find myself constantly starting new projects. I use projects to take the focus off of my brokenness. I see myself doing that because it takes my mind off grief, which interferes with my healing process because I'm not focused on what I have going on in my life at that given time. It's normal to have mixed emotions when someone close to you dies. After the initial shock, one begins to go into a state of emotionlessness and your body is like an empty capsule like a zombie from a walking dead episode. This was a very scary time for me during the death of my husband. I felt cheated that God just wasn't answering my prayers. This feeling was different from when my dad died. I was surrounded by family and several of my siblings were still living at home not to say that I was in my self-centered teenage years. The focus then was on my mother assuring that she was going to make it through this difficult time. As a teenager, I thought that everything was fine, however, the tables were turned. Now, my mom is the head of the household which means the financial situation has changed. My mom was used to managing her money and my dad was responsible for the household which meant things changed because we now needed a new Chief Financial Officer so I assigned myself to the job which became my first project. This project was to assist my mom with getting financial responsibilities handled in a timely fashion. I know you are probably thinking that this was a big responsibility for a senior in high school, however, we needed to survive. We made it through those difficult times. I just want to be irresponsible. When I think I am irresponsible, my heavenly father rescues me. I've always had that brother's keeper type syndrome by making other people's issues mine. I moved over 600 miles away to Delaware and I'm still concerned about what's happening in Cincinnati. I was wondering if my nieces and nephews were doing well and, by this time, my mom had remarried so that was another concern. My older siblings were able to move on with their lives as usual. They were raising their children and taking care of their households. I was able to travel with friends to Freaknik in Atlanta and the Greek in Philadelphia, which are large college gatherings where everyone mingles and parties for a weekend. I felt like I was moving forward and living my best life until I reach another milestone realizing that my dad isn't here to witness it, envying the milestones he was able to share in my siblings' life that he was never here to share in mine. My son never had the opportunity to receive one of my dad's infamous nicknames. My dad would look at my niece or nephew and in an instant come up with a nickname like *Hissie;* my niece with a very squeaky and high pitch voice, *Hagatha*, my niece that's rough around the edges and he named my nephew who was born with no hair at all and never really grew any hair *Kojak* after the television sitcom starring Telly Savalas. I never ever got to have those enjoyable times that my siblings were able to share with my dad. I'm always so concerned about others' wellbeing, that I can't focus on my own. This is the distraction needed to keep my focus off of the thing that was making me angry, so I never was able to completely heal. I was so preoccupied that I was depressed and didn't even know it. I never slowed down long enough to let depression settle in completely. Around the Christmas holiday, I would find myself shopping a lot to take my focus off the hurt that comes with the holiday, considering that was the period that my dad had died. As the years went by, I found that I was celebrating the holiday so I wouldn't deprive my son of the happy moments. It had gotten so bad that my sister would call me the Grinch. As soon as I thought that I was doing better. I would travel during the Christmas holiday so I wouldn't have to decorate the house. My son and I would get to spend the holiday with our family in Cincinnati thinking he would enjoy the company because it was usually him and I in Delaware. When I think that I'm progressing and moving forward into acceptance mode, another family member or a close friend would die. This would trigger old emotions. A year later, when my younger cousin got married, as I helped her get dressed for her big day, steaming her dress and all the hustle and bustle and excitement that takes place before, during and after the wedding, I had overwhelming emotions that I had to suppress by constantly moving and occupying myself by helping the wedding party, wearing the mask that I'm ok only after three months of my husband's death. I had the same effect when I thought picking my husband's jeep up from the repair shop would be easy breezy, however, once I turned on the radio and heard the music from one of his favorite mixed cd's blasting from the CD player, I found myself overwhelmed with emotions reliving the different events we shared on the drives to work or just hanging out. I find myself driving his jeep every opportunity I get to spend time in his presence by sitting in the drivers' seat that he occupied so many days and nights. Some nights, I have to resist the urge of going outside sitting in my husband's Jeep and listen to his radio just to be close to him. Before putting on my shoes, I remind myself that I live in the Medical District aka AVONDALE and that might not be safe. These days, that might not be safe in WEST CHESTER either. If I could reverse time, I would do it in heartbeat just to have more time with my dad and husband. If you guys are sharing time with your family and friends, cherish the moments that you share with one another. Complete the project even if the end result doesn't look like the picture, if it leans to one side or even leaks after your spouse says it's fixed. DON'T SWEAT THE SMALL STUFF!!!!!!!!!

Your Journey
Your Distractions

Scripture:

1Peter 5:7, Cast all your anxiety on him because he cares for you

THE INVISIBLE STRING

Some researchers believe that there are five stages of grief and others believe there are seven. One thing we all can agree on is that grief exists and occurs after some kind of tragedy takes place in our life. The stages of grief are **shock**, when you first learn of the death of a loved one, **denial**, when you deny the fact that your loved one has died, **anger**, when you lash out at others for the death of your loved one, **guilt**, when you feel you could've done more or it should have been you, **bargaining,** when you are making a trade-off, **depression**, when you isolate yourself after the death of a loved one and **acceptance**, when you make a conscious decision to move forward after the death of a loved one. Knowing the stages of grief helps you to understand the abnormality that comes with grief and that it is actually healthy to feel the numbness.

Shock

The initial shock of the loved one's death leaves you numb and in disbelief. I can remember when my dad died my senior year in high school. I remember it as if it were yesterday. It was a cold winter night in January, we were getting ready for church. Growing up, every year after New Year's Eve all night service, our church hosted a six-week revival. We would have churches from New York, New Jersey, Savannah Georgia, and Atlanta Georgia as well as from the Greater Cincinnati area. As my younger sister, Lene, my best friend, Tonya, and I were getting dressed in my bedroom on the third floor of our family home, Tonya was always telling some type of story and we would mock the elders in the church shouting (as some people say catching the Holy Ghost). As we were laughing and having a good time, we looked up and noticed red flashing lights outside of the bedroom window and heard the sirens blasting and getting louder and louder. The sirens abruptly stopped, and the red flashing lights were shining brightly through my bedroom window. We realized that the firetruck and ambulance stopped in front of our house. We ran down the four flights of stairs to see what was going on. As we reached the bottom of the steps and looked down the narrow hallway into the entrance of my parents' bedroom, we saw a gang of paramedics and firemen exiting the room. As I poked my head around the corner of the hallway, I saw my older brother Elvin standing at my mom's side comforting her.

I can only remember her saying "I was only in the kitchen for a second and when I returned, he was gone." I looked in the bedroom and I saw my grandmother standing at the foot of the hospital bed rubbing my dad's legs as she repeatedly said "Dell, don't leave me, Dell don't leave me". Words from a mother to her child. That was January 8th, 1986. I carried on as if nothing changed. Days went by and it was time to attend my dad's funeral. I was still fine because I could physically see my dad although he might not be able to respond to my questions. However, the service was moving forward, and it was time to go to the cemetery. The shock kicked in as I was standing at the gravesite on a cold winter day freezing my butt off. I heard the words "as we commit this body back to the earth, ashes to ashes, dust to dust." It was then and only then that I realized that my daddy was never coming back. That night when we returned home, we still had family members lagging around in the small living room spilling over into the dining room, hallway, and kitchen. I went to my bedroom where I could be alone and that's when the main water break began. I cried until my throat was super dry and there weren't any tears or sound left. I began the emotional rollercoaster ride of anger when my dad died. Angry that he wasn't going to witness any of my milestones: graduation from high school/college, first job, purchasing of my first car/home, birth of my son and my wedding day. Not to forget due to his illness, he wasn't able to attend my Debutante Ball, a way to introduce your daughter to society. I see it as my first event of my dad entrusting me to another male be it for one minute, an hour or a day.

Anger

This makes me angry even over thirty years later, I find myself getting angry at God. Why am I angry? I'm angry because I didn't have the opportunity of relaxing as a teenager and as a young adult because I had to be the responsible one. I wanted to live carefree and have my dad here to bail me out when I got in over my head. Like the time when my dad would get a crew together, usually my brothers and maybe some of their friends, to move my sisters in their apartment. My sisters, Nessa, and Lena, were in their twenties when they decided to move into their own apartment. My dad got the moving truck and my brothers early on a Saturday morning and they disassembled my sisters' beds to be moved into their new apartment. It was like a warehouse assembly line and my father was the foreman shouting out orders from the inside of the house. Once the furniture was taken outside, my dad would be on the truck telling my brothers how to stack the furniture so that all of the objects would fit properly. Once the truck was packed, my dad would jump in the driver's seat of the truck and shout, "Everybody but a wagon body, every soul but a shoe sole!" My brothers would run to their respective vehicles to ride over to my sisters' apartment to unload the truck. Another example of my dad's love for his children came when my older siblings got stranded somewhere and their dad was to the rescue. I had to call AAA. I was very angry that my dad would not be alive to participate in the milestones of my life. Growing up, I watched my dad share in these special meetings with my siblings. He participated in my sister's debutante ball and she was able to have her first dance with my dad. That is something that I never had the pleasure of experiencing. That night is such a beautiful experience hanging out with young ladies that you meet from different areas of Cincinnati and school districts. These are young ladies that you have built a sisterhood with that you may not have ever met in life. Even while getting dressed, we were joking around and complimenting each on their ball gowns. We would wait for our names to be announced and the waltz with our dads and he hands you off to your escort. It's like him trusting another male to take care of you. I wouldn't know.

What I do know is the ANGER I feel at this very moment. I'm angry at God for cheating me out of my HAPPILY EVER AFTER. Must I always be the sacrificial lamb? Why is it always me? I remember when we had that dreadful family meeting at the hospital. The nurse came into the hospital room and said, "The doctor wants to schedule a meeting with you and the family regarding the next steps for your husband's care". I schedule the meeting and called our siblings and my son to attend the meeting. The doctor came in and explained his prognosis of my husband's condition. He then proceeds with the option as we move forward. He asked if I wanted to take him off of the respirator. The family and I made the painful decision to remove him from the respirator. This was the scariest and most crucial decision that I had to make so far in my life. Angry at God, the doctor, my husband, and myself. There is nothing wrong with being angry. You have lost someone dear to you. I had to recognize that I was not myself, I had to get used to a new normal being single again. Anger is normal, but is it going to be constructive or destructive? LET IT OUT!!!!!!!!!

Depression

Growing up in an African American household in the 70s and 80s, you might have heard of someone using the word *depression* in a sentence about someone they knew or discussing a soap opera episode which was popular during that era. However, you rarely heard them use it when it pertained to an African American individual. They were so used to dealing with life's situations that they would describe it as *having a hard time* and would usually end with *you better pray about it*. Having a spiritual relationship and being able to have a little talk with Jesus made it right. That is why so many of us are dealing with depression and don't even know it. You ask how I know this to be true. I can say it's true. I am living through it NOW. My husband died on June 12th, 2019. I was a wife for a whole ten months. I was supposed to grow old with my husband, travel with the grandchildren and live our best life. I walk around daily going through life as if nothing traumatic has taken place in my life. When people ask how I'm doing, I tell them that I'm fine and taking it day by day. But honestly, I want to scream from the top of my lungs," **I'm not ok! My husband died ten months after we got married. I'm a fifty-one-year-old widow, how the hell do you think I feel?"** But instead, I continued on working, serving others, and going through life as what I think is normal. I would find myself constantly moving nonstop. Hence, the chapter *I'm not your Superwoman*. Doing things for everyone else to keep busy so I wouldn't feel the pain and fall into a depressive state of mind. When I isolate myself or find myself alone sometimes depression would come like a big tidal wave and sometimes, I wouldn't even notice that there was a tidal wave until it has come and gone. When the tides are overwhelming, I usually feel myself coming to a breaking point like I'm standing at the end of a bridge just ready to jump just waiting on a strong gust of wind to help me fly away. Then there's a touch on my shoulder and a light whisper in my ear. A voice with great power says, "THIS IS NOT THE END; IT IS THE BEGINNING OF SOMETHING NEW".

DENIAL

Denial is the refusal to accept the facts of the loss, either consciously or unconsciously. There is a period when you are in a state of refusal that death is going to take place, or it has already taken place. I had a serious case of denial. I remember the experience oh so well. I never thought that I would experience something so terrifying. It was late at night or early in the morning when I was awakened from a dream that was very authentic, I was standing in front of my husband laying in a coffin with a dark gray suit, white shirt and a maroon tie and handkerchief. I sat straight up in the bed, looked over at my husband and checked his respiration to assure that he was still breathing. That was God's way of preparing me for a life changing event. I was in such denial that I was like that was just a bad dream. The next morning, as I prepared for work, my husband and chauffeur would grab my work bag and lunch, make his way to the car, warm the car and patiently wait until I came out so he could drive me off to work. He would pick up his work crew to begin any appointments he had scheduled for the day. As a contractor, his schedule was more flexible than mine. This one time, we started our day off as usual. He dropped me off at work and he told me to call him early if I wanted him to bring me lunch. As lunchtime was approaching, I informed my co-workers that I was calling David to bring me lunch and if they wanted something. We ordered lunch from Camp Washington Chili which is a diner like restaurant in Cincinnati that serves pretty much everything from breakfast food, double decker sandwiches, salads, etc. David delivered lunch and appeared to be feeling fine. I continued working through the rest of the day. I received an unwarranted phone call from David. We called each other periodically throughout the day. He was saying that he wasn't feeling well, and he wasn't able to drive. He wanted to know if there was any way I could have a co-worker drop me off. One of my coworkers was able to drop me off at home. During the ride home, she asked if *Brother David* was doing ok. I explained to her that he wasn't feeling well. When I arrived home, David was in the bed complaining of severe stomach pains. David wasn't a complainer, so I guess I ignored God's sign once again.

My husband always had a hearty appetite and was always chipper. Suddenly, my husband wouldn't eat any food and it was difficult for him to drink water. I would prepare him a cup of immune tea for him to drink in the morning, before I would leave for work, trying to get him to at least drink liquids. These failing attempts were alarming, and he would complain that the pain was worsening. I decided that David should go to the emergency room to be evaluated. As we drove to the ER, every bump in the road would send David into a frenzy of pain. I would apologize every time we would hit a bump in the road. We arrive at the ER and it is extremely overflowing with people. I went into the ER lobby to retrieve a wheelchair to assist David because the pain was so excruciating that he could hardly walk. When he got in the chair, he laid his head on his knees to relieve some of the pain. If you ever experienced an individual battling cancer, they explain that the cancer usually is not what ends the person's life. I was wondering if my husband may have had appendicitis because he was complaining that the pain was traveling from the stomach to his side. As we patiently waited in the waiting area, my husband was very uncomfortable and in excruciating pain and it seemed as if the minutes were an eternity. He was squirming in the wheelchair trying to get comfortable. Finally, after hours of waiting, we were called back to have his vitals taken only to return to the waiting area to wait even longer and then after more hours of waiting, we were officially assigned an exam room. The nurse enters yelling as if the pain were connected to his hearing. "Mr. Clark, I hear you are having pain, can you tell me where's the pain, how long have you been having the pain, on a scale of one to ten with ten being the highest how would you rate your pain?." My husband never likes to complain and responds that the pain is a level six. I'm raising my eyebrows because with all that he was doing, that pain should've been off the chart!!!! I'm thinking "dude, a level six? We could've stayed home for that." They hooked David to an I.V to get some fluids because he was dehydrated then, they drew blood and ran labs. After waiting for the lab results, he was admitted to the hospital. The next morning, when the doctors were doing rounds, the hospitalist on call for David's oncologist decides to tell me that she thinks it's time to put David on palliative care (comfort care) and she would have pastoral care and the social worker comes to speak with me about my next steps. Not wanting to accept what they were trying to prepare me for (which was the worst), I was staying positive and keeping the faith while the medical professionals were doing their jobs, trying to prepare me for the worst. David spent a couple of days in the hospital. Once they discharged David from the hospital, he had a follow up appointment with his oncologist for his regular treatment. David was beginning to get weaker and weaker. He would ask for a wheelchair when getting out of the car at the Dr.'s office. He was already a thin man, but he had gotten frailer and fragile and was taking multiple stops to catch his breath as he walked from the car to the front door. We were making frequent visits to the hospital and David would be admitted for days at a time for dehydration. After one hospital occurrence, David and I were sitting in the bedroom having a normal conversation, I was lying across the bed and he was sitting in the chair near the patio looking out the door. He looks at me and says, "I want that picture of me with you and your mom on my obituary." I was furious!!!!! I jumped off the bed and stormed out of the bedroom shouting "If you want to plan your own funeral, you can go tomorrow and make plans and have just the way you want it." Yet in denial. I believe that individuals are given a sign from God letting them know when the end time is drawing near. They are trying to prepare the people closest to them for what's getting ready to take place. It is a time that we all dread so we selfishly want the person to stay around. Knowing my husband, if he is not at a hundred percent, he doesn't want to be a bother or burden to anyone. As bad as it hurts, we have to let them go.

Acceptance

Acceptance is making the conscious decision to move forward. Accepting this traumatic life changing event doesn't mean I'm celebrating it. You are accepting that a broken heart can't be seen. It's one thing when you break your arm and it's put in a cast to fix the injury. Unlike when you just see me walking around smiling and trying to mend the broken heart that's in many pieces. I'm making the decision to move forward, taking the next steps to getting my life back on track to being a healthier individual. I began by working from the inside out, not forgetting my dad or husband, but making a mental note that it is something that's beyond my control and I must keep living. I can think back on the enjoyable times we shared together and the stronger I become, the more I can help others through their grieving process. If I allowed myself to stay angry, or upset every time something beyond my control happens, then I'm not able to move forward. So, I decided to accept that this has happened now, and I had to make it better. The first thing I began to try is to commit some time for prayer and meditation, spending some alone time with God who is the creator of the Universe. I was spending a lot of time alone anyway so why not invite God (higher being, or whoever you reference your prayers) into my space? I joined a prayer circle as a support system. Every morning at 6, we are on the telephone praying for one another and for others. I joined this group during my husband's illness. I would call in on the telephone line and make my request known for my husband's healing to take place believing that God was going to heal my husband's body. Although my husband wasn't healed, I faithfully joined the 6am call every Monday through Friday to pray and help someone else. The second thing I started was changing my eating habits being mindful of what I put into my temple. I watched my husband's poor eating habits for years of being a carnivore, so I decided that I was going to eliminate meat from my diet and focus on getting my body into a more alkaline state to stay ailment free. I began to drink more spring water, eat fruits and vegetables, exercise and use herbal supplements. This was my way of saying that my husband and father both missed important life changing events in my life so I wanted to do everything in my control to ensure that I would be here to see my grandchildren grow into adulthood and develop into what God has destined them to be.

Your Journey
Navigating

Your Journey
The Power of Nooooo

Your Journey
Navigating

Your Journey
Navigating

Scripture:

1John 1:9: If we confess our sins, he is faithful and just and will forgive us our sins and purify us from all unrighteousness.

IN SEARCH OF HEALING

What is healing? It is simply the process of becoming healthy again. Is there a time limit or a proper way an individual has to complete the healing process? Healing from the death of a loved one or a friend isn't like having surgery and the surgeon gives you a time frame that you should recuperate from your injury. Unlike surgery, grief can be like an ocean tide. Sometimes, the tide comes in heavy and it's overwhelming and other times, it's hardly noticeable. It's not something you get over, but something you learn to manage constructively. You have to ask yourself the question, "do I want to suffer this pain for the rest of my life, or do I want to move forward?" I chose to move forward so I began to take the proper steps towards managing my grief, so I could move forward.

How do you manage the grief? The grief is managed through alone time as well as giving myself permission to grieve, taking care of myself, surrounding myself with friends and family, spirituality and meditation, trying to find meaning in the loss and deciding on the next stage in life.

Alone time is my friend. I use this time to focus on the good times I shared with my husband. I use this alone time to cry, to lean into my grief by releasing anger towards the situation, and to ask God questions. I don't know about you, but I don't like to display vulnerability or weakness in front of others. During this time, I find myself scrolling through my phone watching videos that we've made throughout the years. This gives me the opportunity to reflect and hear his voice once again. My husband wasn't very fond of social media. He really disliked when I would annoy him and video it on Snapchat. I love watching those videos and being amazed at how he developed into a "Snapchatter" or appeased me long enough to participate in the videos by my side. I watched our wedding video multiple times sometimes, weeping, other times I observe something that I didn't see previously.

I don't really talk with my friends that are married due to the feelings that arise when I talk with them. Some of my friends have been married for over twenty years and get to have a happily ever after. I am not resentful or envious of their relationship, I just wonder why I wasn't able to have happiness ever after life. It's like being single all over again and you don't want to be the third wheel or listen to what your friend and their husband or significant other are planning. I recently picked my husband's jeep up from the repair shop. When I sat in his seat, I immediately reminisced about the times we shared in the jeep.

Times when he would be sitting in my work's parking awaiting my exit from the building. My coworkers would stop and converse with David on their walk to their vehicles. Afterwards, they would text or call me to inform me that David was outside waiting, not knowing that he has already sent me a notification through a text or phone call. My co-workers will jokingly tell me not to have Brother David outside waiting. On occasion, my co-workers will tell me how much they miss seeing David outside waiting in the parking lot as they exit the building. This makes me smile and lets me know that although they weren't family, they were also grieving the loss of my husband, just in a different manner. I was cleaning the inside of his truck, trying to remove the debris and dust from the repairs and sitting in the sun, spraying the windshield with a glass cleaner and I could do nothing but smile as I thought of him sitting in the driver's seat listening to his music and bumping his head up and down to the beat as he wipes down the windshield or the dashboard as he admires its shine. Every unwarrantable memory that makes me cry or smile is a new step toward healing. I also had to grow up. I hadn't realized that I hadn't actually healed from the death of my dad. I would start many projects and not complete them. I think about it now as those were ways to occupy myself and once, I get bored, I would stop and move on to something else. Writing this book has allowed me to share my feelings. Sharing has allowed me to be transparent and putting it all on the table for everyone to read has lifted a burden that is leading to healing. I hoped that my story could be healing for others.

Prayer for Mind Cleansing & Clarity

Heavenly Father, I come to you now in the Name of my Lord and Savior Jesus Christ. Lord Jesus, I ask you to wash my mind with the Blood of Jesus and cleanse out all darkness and all thoughts that are contrary to Your Will and destiny for my life. I ask you Lord Jesus to shut any doors that need to be shut whether spiritual or natural, and to open any doors that need to be opened whether spiritual or natural in my life. Heavenly Father, I ask you to give me clarity of vision, clarity of sight, clarity of thought, clarity of mind, clarity of knowing and hearing Your Voice. In Jesus Name I pray. Amen!

Your Journey
Your Search

When you can't find the words to pray here are some prayers from the LITTLE RED PRAYER BOOK.

Prayer for a person who is grieving the loss of a loved one

Please help me in this time of loss of _____. I seem to be frozen with this overwhelming grief. I don't understand why my life is filled with this pain and heartache. But I turn my eyes to you as I seek to find the strength to trust in your faithfulness. You Lord are a God of comfort and love and I ask you to help me to patiently wait on you and not despair; I will quietly wait for your peace. My heart is crushed, but I know that you will not abandon me. Please show me your compassion, Lord. Help me through this pain so that I will hope in you again. I believe your promise in Your Word to send me fresh mercy each day. Though I can't see past today, I trust your love will never fail me. Jesus, you came to heal the brokenhearted and my heart is broken today Lord, and only you can heal my sorrow over losing _____. I ask You, Lord to comfort me because you love me and have promised me everlasting consolation and hope through your grace. Blessed be to God, even the Father of our Lord Jesus Christ, the Father of mercies, and the God of all comfort; who comforts me in all my tribulations, that I may be protected from any trouble and hurt as I walk with you, Lord, through the grief of losing _____. In Jesus Name I pray. Amen

Prayer for One Who Has Lost a Spouse

O' Heavenly Father, I am now in the shadow of great loneliness. My helpmate has been taken from me. Yet I submit in holy faith to your divine will. I know that you loved _____ and that they are now in Heaven rejoicing with you (2 Colossians 5:8). Lord, right now I don't know what to do with the rest of my life. Please lead and guide me in this time of uncertainty. Help me Lord, to seek out opportunities to help those less fortunate than myself so that I can be a blessing to them. Help me to keep from feeling sorry for myself in my present condition. Keep my heart alive with your love for my neighbor, so I can carry on your work of love in this world. One day I know I will be reunited with ____ in Heaven, where we both will worship you for all eternity. Amen.

Lora Ward Clark

Prayer for Someone Missing a Spouse That Has Passed

Heavenly Father, I know that grieving is a process and healing of my loss will take time. This has been so difficult, Lord. ____ was a part of my life for so many years. Everyday Lord, the simplest task reminds me of what's been lost. Lord, I ask you to make this emptiness that I am feeling become less every day. Show me Lord, to use this time in a way that I can glorify you. God, I know that I am not alone, that you are here with me in this loneliness. But Lord, please forgive me if I still feel alone at times Hebrews 4:15). I thank you Lord that you will not leave me nor forsake me in this time of sorrow even if sometimes I forget to acknowledge that you are indeed here. Lord, You are a God of love please be with me as I try to go forth missing ____ in every way; at night, at dinner, when I turn to ____ to speak and they aren't there. Be with me, Lord as I try to have a life without my love, my friend, and my companion. Keep me strong, safe, and supported as I journey on alone abiding in you. In Jesus Name I ask these things. Amen

CONCLUSION

I pray that this book reaches everyone that God has intended. I pray that as I share my journey with you, I am able to grab your hand and guide you through yours. Proverbs 24:16 says "though the righteous fall seven times, they rise again, but the wicked stumble when calamity strikes." The wicked falls just as the righteous person does, only the wicked gives up and never gets up, being defeated. The strength is found in the struggle. Grief is just a trial that we all must encounter throughout our lifetime more than once. Once you encounter grief, what will be your outcome? Will you be the wicked person that stays down, or will you be the righteous person that falls, gets up, dust off and keeps it moving? Every time you get up, you're stronger than you were before. Don't get discouraged because it seems as if you are constantly being knocked down. There is a reason and season for every situation we encounter, but when it's time for you to come out of the fire (situation) you are going to shine like pure gold. Gold has to go through a process and pressure to increase its value. I'm not saying it's going to be easy but it's going to be right. Every time you take a step, a different burden falls off. Just keep the faith and one day, you are going to wake up and feel lighter. Things are going to look brighter. You will look back on that moment and think, "WOW! How did I ever make it through that? I know because through this journey, I constantly reflect on how God is delivering me through it all. There's a song that Marvin Sapp sings that is on my healing playlist. It says "I'm thankful for all the good, bad, the ugly great and small. I'm so grateful that I'm still standing tall." This song has blessed my life along with others. Through my trials and tribulations, from watching my dad's health decline at 16, watching my infant son through his near death experience at 25, and burying my husband of ten months at 51, I could have thrown in the towel, called it quits and laid under a rock and died. That's not my story and I don't want it to be yours. I took my bumps and bruises and kept it pushing. I put some skin in the game with my bruised heel and all. In the words of Sarah Jakes Roberts "I might be walking with a limp; I might be crawling but I'm coming out." I AM THE RIGHTEOUS every time I fall, I get up stronger. I get strength from sharing my story, praying, and saying my affirmations. Affirming God's word over my life and family. These words speak to my spirit, body, and soul, and will constantly change the atmosphere as well as your life. Faith comes by hearing and hearing by the word of God. I pray that God speaks a word over your life through these affirmations that will assist you in your healing process.

APPENDIX:

Discussion Questions

1. How have others suggested that you need to "get over it" and move on? What do you want to say to them when they tell you this?

2. How has your grief disrupted an area of your life (work, school, church, relationships)?

3. If you tried to lean into your grief, how would your grief experience be different?

4. How would you benefit from putting off a decision?

5. If you decided to write a grief letter. What would you tell friends and family that you need from them?

6. Finish the sentence "My life will never be the same again because……."

7. Describe a time when you realized your grief was affecting you more than you previously thought it was.

Invisible String Chart

What's Holding You Back	What are your next steps	What are you going to do to move forward

AFFIRMATIONS:

There is but one power in the universe that's God almighty power and it works through me in me and around me and it goes before me to work things out for my good

I declare that my God is preserving what he has ordained for me and he will lead me into it. Malachi 3:11; Joshua 11:6; Psalms 140:4; Ephesians 2:10

I declare that through God, the battle is already won. 1 Samuel 17:47

I believe God has sent his word and it will not return void. Isaiah 55:11

I expect God's Mercy and Grace on me today. Lamentations 3:22-23

I expect God's Favor and Blessings on me today. Psalms 5:12; Jeremiah 29:11

I believe God has given me his Abundant Life. John 10:10

I am healed by the stripes of Jesus. 1 Peter 2:25; Isaiah 53:6

I declare that God has given us Divine Healing and Divine Health. Matthew 8:2-3; Isaiah 53:5

I DECLARE THAT WE WON THE VICTORY!!!!! 1 Corinthians 15:57-58

WHAT TO LOOK FOR IN A THERAPIST

1. Do they show warmth and acceptance, **empathy**, and a focus on others, not themselves?
2. Can your therapist communicate to you in a language that you understand?
3. Is this someone who allows you to feel that you can have a good working relationship and that your faith in this person won't be betrayed?
4. Do you feel that the therapist cares about your goals in therapy and is willing to work with you to set goals that both of you agree on?
5. Flexibility
6. Inspiration of hope and **optimism** about your chances of improvement.

ABOUT THE AUTHOR

Lora Ward-Clark is an educator, writer, and first-time author of the new book THE SKY FALLS TWICE "Navigating through the stages of grief". Lora wrote this book as a testimony to the fact that the devastating loss of loved ones shouldn't stop you from living. She shares skills that help build fortitude through deceleration and careful grief management. With compassion, Lora has helped others to their feet during some of life's most traumatic experiences. Lora has a B.A. in Occupational and Vocational Education from Delaware State University and she currently resides in Cincinnati with her family.

www.ingramcontent.com/pod-product-compliance
Lightning Source LLC
Chambersburg PA
CBHW031653040426
42453CB00006B/298